Focus on Opiates

Focus on Opiates
A Drug-Alert Book

Susan DeStefano
Illustrated by David Neuhaus

TWENTY-FIRST CENTURY BOOKS
FREDERICK, MARYLAND

Published by
Twenty-First Century Books
38 South Market Street
Frederick, Maryland 21701

Printed in the United States of America

10 9 8 7 6 5 4 3 2 1

Library of Congress Cataloging in Publication Data

DeStefano, Susan
Focus on Opiates
Illustrated by David Neuhaus

(A Drug-Alert Book)
Summary: Examines the social and medical background of
opium use, emphasizing its history as a drug with legitimate
applications and as a powerful and dangerous illegal narcotic.
1. Opium habit—Juvenile literature.
2. Opium habit—United States—Juvenile literature.
3. Narcotics—Juvenile literature.
[1. Opium. 2. Narcotics. 3. Drugs. 4. Drug abuse.]
I. Neuhaus, David, ill. II. Title.
III. Series: The Drug-Alert Series.
HV5816.D47   1991
362.29'3'0973—dc20   90-11157   CIP   AC
ISBN 0-941477-91-6

Table of Contents

Introduction

"Baby Saved by Miracle Drug!" "Drug Bust at Local School!" Headlines like these are often side by side in your newspaper, or you may hear them on the evening news. This is confusing. If drugs save lives, why are people arrested for having and selling them?

The word "drug" is part of the confusion. It is a word with many meanings. The drug that saves a baby's life is also called a medicine. The illegal drugs found at the local school have many names—names like pot, speed, and crack. But one name for all of these illegal drugs is dope.

Some medicines you can buy at your local drugstore or grocery store, and there are other medicines only a doctor can get for you. But whether you buy them yourself or need a doctor to order them for you, medicines are made to get you healthy when you are sick.

Dope is not for sale in any store. You can't get it from a doctor. Dope is bought from someone called a "dealer" or a "pusher" because using, buying, or selling dope is against the law. That doesn't stop some people from using dope. They say they do it to change the way they feel. Often, that means they are trying to run away from their problems. But when the dope wears off, the problems are still there—and they are often worse than before.

There are three drugs we see so often that we sometimes forget they really are drugs. These are alcohol, nicotine, and caffeine. Alcohol is in beer, wine, and liquor. Nicotine is found in cigarettes, cigars, pipe tobacco, and other tobacco products. Caffeine is in coffee, tea, soft drinks, and chocolate. These three drugs are legal. They are sold in stores. But that doesn't mean they are always safe to use. Alcohol and nicotine are such strong drugs that only adults are allowed to buy and use them. And most parents try to keep their children from having too much caffeine.

Marijuana, cocaine, alcohol, nicotine, caffeine, medicines: these are all drugs. All drugs are alike because they change the way our bodies and minds work. But different drugs cause different changes. Some help, and some harm. And when they aren't used properly, even helpful drugs can harm us.

Figuring all this out is not easy. That's why The Drug-Alert Books were written: so you will know why certain drugs are used, how they affect people, why they are dangerous, and what laws there are to control them.

Knowing about drugs is important. It is important to you and to all the people who care about you.

David Friedman, Ph.D.
Consulting Editor

Dr. David Friedman is Associate Professor of Physiology and Pharmacology and Assistant Dean of Research Development at the Bowman Gray School of Medicine, Wake Forest University.

The Opiate Problem

The bright rays of the sun beat down on a remote hillside in Burma, in Southeast Asia. Here, in this dry, poor soil, miles from any village or town, a beautiful flower blooms. Its white, ruffled petals unfold. Their edges are tinged with violet. This is the white opium poppy. And, soon, for as far as the eye can see, row after row of these beautiful flowers will open their blossoms to the sun.

But the opium poppy is more than just a beautiful flower. It is also the source of a powerful drug.

- It is a drug so powerful that people once thought it was a gift from the gods.

- It is a drug so powerful that it can ease the terrible pain of cancer.

- It is a drug so powerful that it can destroy the people who use it.

The drug is opium.

9

Opium, and other drugs made from opium, are called opiates. Some of these opiate drugs are morphine, codeine, and heroin. Like most other drugs, opiates change the way the body works. Like many other drugs, opiates also change the way the brain works. They change the way we think, feel, and behave. Drugs that act on the brain to change the way it works are called psychoactive drugs. Alcohol, marijuana, and cocaine are psychoactive drugs. Opium, morphine, codeine, and heroin are also psychoactive drugs.

Like many drugs, opiates can help people to feel better when they are sick or hurt. They can be used as medicine. But like many other drugs, opiates can be very dangerous, too. If not used properly, they can harm the body and brain.

Until now, you may not have heard very much about opiates. When parents and teachers discuss the drug problem with young people, they usually talk about alcohol, marijuana, and cocaine. But you should know the facts about opiates, too. Why? Because you have to live and grow up in a world where opiate use exists. Because, one day, you may have to make a decision about using these drugs. Because the more you know about drugs, the easier it is to say "No" to them.

It is important for you to understand what opiates are. It is important to know how they can be useful as medicine and how they can harm individuals, families, and all of society. It is important for you to understand the opiate problem.

What is the opiate problem?

A popular television news program focused on just how harmful an opiate like heroin can be. In 1990, the program took its camera to a busy city park in Switzerland. The place is called Needle Park. As the eye of the camera swept around the park, one thing became very clear. This wasn't the kind of park where families go to picnic. This wasn't the kind of park where kids go to play. This was a park overflowing with drug users. On every bench, beside every bush, people were buying, selling, and using drugs.

The camera stopped. Slowly, it focused on one teenage boy. He was sitting on the grass, leaning against a tree. His hair was dirty, and his skin was pale. He was very thin. One of his shirt sleeves was rolled up. Ugly sores and scabs trailed down the inside of his arm.

The camera came closer. The boy didn't seem to notice or care that he was being watched. He stuck a needle into his arm. It was a needle filled with heroin. The boy's head fell back against the tree. His eyelids drooped. And all the while the needle dangled from his arm.

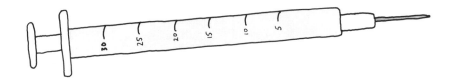

The boy is a "junkie." Heroin is also called "junk," and a heroin user is sometimes called a junkie. A junkie lives for heroin. Nothing else matters. Heroin does that to people.

A heroin junkie, like this boy, looks sick and miserable. He doesn't eat well, sometimes going for days without food. He doesn't care if he sees his family or friends. Most likely, his family and friends would rather not see him. Yet none of these things bothers him. The only thing he thinks about when he opens his eyes each day is heroin. The only thing he cares about is heroin. Heroin rules his life. Heroin *is* his life.

Now, let's switch the scene.

Imagine that you have gone with your parents to visit your grandfather in the hospital. He has just had a serious operation. You can hear him moaning softly, and you know the pain must be very bad. Soon, a nurse comes into the room. She says she's going to give your grandfather some morphine. Neither your father nor your mother says anything. You are shocked. You know that morphine can be a dangerous drug. You know that drugs can hurt the body and brain. You are surprised that anyone would give your grandfather drugs.

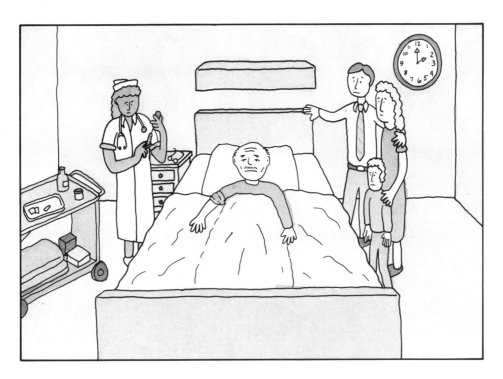

"Why doesn't someone stop her? Isn't anyone worried that my grandfather is using drugs?" you wonder. "Doesn't anyone care?"

Of course, your parents care. So do the doctor and nurse. They know that morphine is a medicine that can ease your grandfather's pain. Soon after the nurse gives him the shot of morphine, your grandfather is able to talk to you and your parents. His pain has been relieved. It seems almost incredible.

Your grandfather's doctor told the nurse to give him the shot of morphine. The doctor also told the nurse exactly how much morphine to give your grandfather. This was probably just enough to ease his pain. The doctor knows that with less pain, your grandfather will recover more quickly or, at least, be more comfortable. And the doctor also knows that patients almost never become addicted to morphine or other opiates when these drugs are given to relieve pain.

Now, let's switch the scene again.

Picture yourself in bed at home with a very bad cold. Last night, you coughed so hard that your throat hurt and your chest ached. You coughed so much that you didn't get any sleep. This morning your mother took you to the doctor. The doctor said that your cough was serious and that you needed medicine and lots of rest to get better. Then, the doctor wrote out a prescription for a cough medicine with codeine. Codeine is a very mild opiate. But the codeine in the cough medicine is strong enough to quiet your cough and let you get a good night's sleep.

How can something that helps people get better also be harmful? How can something that eases your grandfather's pain and calms a bad cough also hurt other people? How can something that comes from such a lovely flower lead a teenage boy to a terrible drug habit?

That's the opiate problem. Opiate drugs can be helpful. Opiate drugs can be harmful. A drug that can be very useful as a medicine can be very dangerous, too.

This book will help you understand the opiate problem. You will learn important facts about opiates and why people use them. You will learn that opiates change the way the brain and the body work. You will learn how people have used opiates in the past and why they are a problem today.

And you will learn how to make a smart, safe decision about opiates. You will learn how to say "No" to harmful drug use and how to say "Yes" to your health and happiness.

What Are Opiates?

The most well known opiate drugs are opium, morphine, codeine, and heroin. Some opiate drugs come directly from the opium poppy. Other opiates are made in a laboratory. Some opiate drugs are used as medicine today. Others have no medical use. Some opiate drugs are stronger than other ones. It is important for you to know the differences among these opiate drugs.

But it is also important for you to know one thing that is the same for each of these drugs: opiates change the way the brain works.

- They change the brain so that an opiate user does not feel pain. Opiates block pain messages from reaching the brain.

- They change the brain so that an opiate user gets a feeling of pleasure. Opiates make people feel peaceful and sleepy.

The scientific name for the opium poppy is *Papaver som-niferum*. It means "the poppy that brings sleep." The opium poppy got its name because opiate drugs ease pain and make people sleepy.

Because opiate drugs change the brain in these ways, they can be very useful as medicines. Doctors know that it helps sick people to be able to stop feeling their pain. It helps them to be able to stop thinking so much about their pain.

But these same changes to the brain mean that opiates can also be very dangerous.

Some people use opiates because they like the feeling of pleasure it gives them. They become very calm and peacefully sleepy. Their troubles seem far away. This feeling makes some people want to take the drug again and again. But after a while they begin to need the drug to feel any pleasure at all. And soon they need the drug just to feel normal. They feel sick without the drug. These people are addicted to opiates.

What is addiction?

Addiction is the constant need or craving for a drug. It means that drug use has changed the way the brain works. The addicted brain wants the feeling it gets from drugs even more than it wants the very things the body needs to survive. The addicted brain no longer gets pleasure from safe, healthy, and nourishing things, like food and sleep. It gets pleasure only from drugs.

How People Take Opiates

Opiates change the way the brain works. In order for them to work, they have to get to the brain. Drugs are carried to the brain in the body's bloodstream. How do opiates get into the bloodstream?

- Some opiates can be eaten or taken in liquid form. They pass slowly from the stomach and intestines into the bloodstream, where they are carried to the brain. This is what happens when people use cough syrup containing codeine or take morphine tablets.

- Some opiates can be smoked. The lungs breathe in the drug and send it on to the bloodstream. This is a quicker way for the drugs to reach the brain, and the effects are much stronger. In the past, millions of people became addicted to smoking opium.

- Some opiates can be injected. They are put directly into a vein with a hypodermic needle. This is the quickest way for opiates to reach the brain, and the effects are the strongest. Patients with severe pain may be given a shot of morphine. Most heroin users give themselves a shot, or "fix," of the drug.

Opiates are made from the seed capsules, or pods, of the opium poppy. The opium poppy grows in the dry soil and warm climate of Southeast and Southwest Asia, Mexico, India, and Turkey. When the flowers of the poppy plants wither and fall, their green seedpods begin to swell. Before the seedpods have a chance to completely ripen and dry out, opium farmers harvest them. With sharp knives, they make several slits in the pods. A milky white juice oozes out of these cuts. When the juice dries and then hardens, it forms a sticky, dark brown substance which can be scraped off the pods. This gummy paste is known as crude opium. Crude opium is used to make the drug opium and the other opiate drugs.

Opium

The drug opium is made by drying out the gummy, dark brown crude opium. When all of the water is dried out of it, crude opium looks like chunks of brown dirt. Some people who use opium crush the brown chunks and smoke it. Other people chew it or sniff it.

Opium was once a very important medicine. In the past, many people took opium for the same problems that we take common medicines today. They took it to relieve minor aches and pains. Doctors gave it to their patients to stop coughs and help them sleep. Opium was also prescribed for diarrhea, a condition which can be very serious and which, in some parts of the world today, causes many deaths every year.

Even when opium was given by a doctor, some people became addicted to it. And the fact that opium was habit-forming was not the only problem. Opium was not a reliable medicine. Sometimes it worked well and helped some patients to feel better. But, other times, opium didn't work at all. It could even make some patients feel worse.

So doctors and scientists kept searching for new opiate medicines. They were searching for opiate drugs that would be less addictive and more reliable. They were searching for an answer to the opiate problem.

Morphine

One of the answers to the opiate problem was morphine.

In 1803, scientists learned that a main chemical in crude opium is morphine. They were able to separate the tiny, white crystals of morphine from the crude opium. Morphine crystals can be crushed and put into capsules to be swallowed. But morphine works better and faster when it is dissolved in water and injected into the bloodstream with a hypodermic needle.

At first, the scientists who discovered morphine thought they had found an answer to the opiate problem. Morphine was a valuable medicine. It was 10 times stronger than opium, it was much more reliable, and it seemed safer to use. Doctors believed that morphine was not as addictive as opium. But they were wrong. Morphine is a very addictive drug.

Today, morphine is still a valuable medicine. It works fast and is quite reliable. Doctors often give morphine injections or pills to patients who are suffering from the terrible pain of cancer or heart disease. In fact, morphine may be one of the first medicines given to someone who has a heart attack.

Morphine is safe when it is used as a medicine. Doctors are careful to use the right amount and to prescribe morphine only when it is really needed. But when it is not used as a medicine, morphine can be a very dangerous drug.

Codeine

The search for an answer to the opiate problem also led scientists to the discovery of codeine. Codeine is a mild opiate. It is only one-tenth as strong as morphine. And it is not nearly as addictive.

Doctors use codeine to treat less serious pain. When you have a broken ankle and take a capsule that contains codeine, you won't feel the pain for several hours. Codeine can bring quick relief from the pain of headaches, toothaches, and other aches and pains.

Doctors also use codeine to stop coughs and to control diarrhea. Like the other opiates, codeine depresses, or slows down, the part of the brain that controls coughing. This is why codeine is able to help quiet a nagging cough. Like the other opiates, codeine also slows down the nerves that help control the movements of the intestines. This is why codeine is able to help stop diarrhea.

Codeine is not as strong as the other opiates, and it is not as addictive. If you are given a medicine with codeine, you don't have to worry that you will get "hooked" on it. However, codeine is still a powerful drug. You can only get it with a doctor's prescription. And some people who are addicted to opiate drugs take codeine when they can't get other opiates.

Heroin

In 1874, scientists once again believed they had solved the opiate problem. In that year, heroin was discovered. Once again, scientists thought they had finally found a strong but safe opiate medicine. And, once again, they were wrong.

Heroin is the strongest of all the drugs that come from crude opium. It is twice as strong as morphine. That's 20 times as strong as crude opium. And it goes to work fast. For these reasons, it is the most addictive of all the opiate drugs.

And it is the most widely used. Heroin is probably used by 90% to 95% of opiate addicts. In the United States alone, there are now between 500,000 and 750,000 heroin addicts.

Today, heroin is the opiate problem. It is a problem for the people who use it. But it is an even bigger problem than that. Heroin use hurts everyone in our society.

Heroin is a white powder made from the drug morphine. The heroin powder can be sniffed or smoked. Or it may be dissolved in water and injected directly into the bloodstream with a hypodermic needle.

There is no medical use of heroin in the United States today, and it is illegal to sell, buy, or use this opiate drug. There is only one reason that people use heroin. They use it to change the way they feel. They use it to get "high."

Opiates belong to a group of drugs known as narcotics. The word "narcotic" comes from a Greek word that means "to make numb" or "to take away feeling." Narcotics slow down, or depress, the way the nervous system works.

There are many questions to answer about opiates:

- Why do opiates work the way they do?

- Why do they give relief from pain?

- Why do they give people a feeling of pleasure?

- And, most important, why do some people who use opiates want to use them over and over again, even when the drugs make them sick?

To answer these and other questions, however, you must first understand how the brain works and how opiate drugs change the way the brain works. When you learn more about the way opiates change the brain, you will begin to understand why opiates are both helpful medicines and dangerous drugs. You will begin to understand the opiate problem.

The Brain

What a big job your brain does for you! Probably even bigger than you think. For example, has anyone ever said to you, "You can solve that math problem. Just use your brain."? Probably. But has anyone ever said to you, "You can kick that ball into the net. Just use your brain."? Or, "You can look at that sunset. Just use your brain."? Probably not. But you need your brain to do those things, too.

Most people already know that the brain helps them to think about and solve math problems. But they don't always realize that the brain also makes it possible for them to kick a soccer ball, see a beautiful sunset, or feel the scratchy touch of sandpaper. The brain makes it possible for them to stay awake or fall asleep, to laugh or cry, to feel sad or happy.

Your brain controls every beat that your heart makes and every breath that your lungs take. Your brain is responsible for every thought and every feeling that you have. It makes it possible for you to be a special person with your very own personality. Your brain makes it possible for you to be you.

It's definitely a big job. It's complicated, too. One way to try to understand all the work that the brain does for you is to think about a puppet and a puppeteer. A puppeteer is the person who controls a puppet. A puppet is often a wooden figure with a head, a body, arms, hands, legs, and feet. All the parts are joined together by strings and soft fabric.

Strings run from the head, shoulders, hands, knees, and feet of the puppet up to a small wooden handle. The puppeteer can control the movements of the puppet by pulling on these strings.

The puppet cannot walk unless the puppeteer pulls the strings that are attached to the puppet's legs. The puppet cannot lift its hand unless the puppeteer pulls the strings attached to the puppet's hand.

The puppet cannot speak unless the puppeteer pulls the strings that are attached to the puppet's jaw and pretends to speak for the puppet.

The puppeteer also controls whether the puppet will act happy or sad, whether the puppet will be angry or calm. The "thoughts" and "feelings" of the puppet are controlled by the puppeteer. The puppeteer gives the puppet a personality of its own. In other words, without the puppeteer, the puppet is nothing but a pile of wood, cloth, and strings.

Your brain could be called your body's puppeteer. Without your brain, you would not be able to move your feet, your arms, or your eyes. Without your brain, your heart wouldn't beat at the right speed and your lungs wouldn't breathe at all.

You wouldn't be able to listen to music or to smell a flower. You wouldn't be able to laugh at a funny joke or cry at a sad story. You wouldn't be able to be you.

A body without a brain is like a puppet without a puppeteer—it's just a pile of skin, muscles, and bones.

What is this puppeteer we call the brain? Let's take a look at the brain.

Although it does such a big, complicated job, your brain is really quite small. The human brain weighs only about three pounds. It is soft and very delicate, too. That's why it needs to be protected by the hard bones of the skull.

You can picture the brain in two parts, a top part and a bottom part. The bottom part of the brain takes care of the kinds of things that help you stay alive. If you're hungry, one area in the bottom part, an area called the hypothalamus, tells you, "Eat." If you're tired, another area called the brain stem tells you, "Go to sleep" (even if you don't really want to).

One special area at the very top of the brain stem controls our feelings of pleasure. That's why this part of the brain is called the pleasure center. When the pleasure center is working, we feel happy or content. In other words, the pleasure center tells us to "Feel good."

The top part of the brain is what makes you so smart. This part of the brain is called the cerebral cortex. A human being's cerebral cortex is much bigger than that of any other animal. The different parts of the cerebral cortex control your senses, movements, and thoughts. They allow your eyes to see; they allow your ears to hear. They allow your muscles to move. They allow your mind to think, to imagine, to dream, to remember, and to understand.

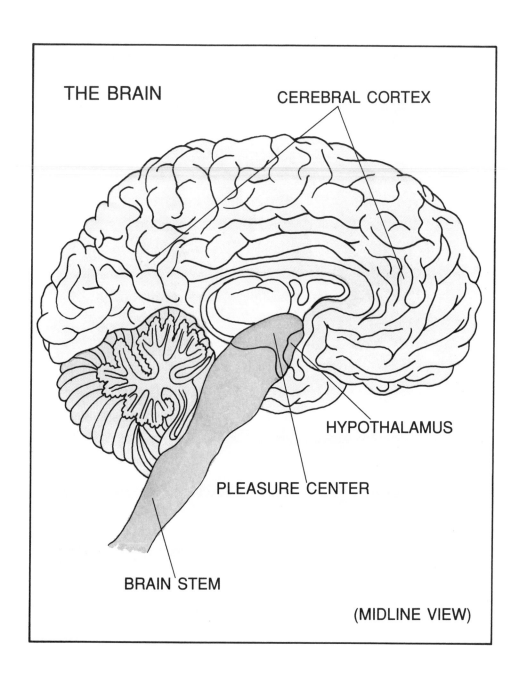

THE BRAIN

CEREBRAL CORTEX

HYPOTHALAMUS

PLEASURE CENTER

BRAIN STEM

(MIDLINE VIEW)

31

The brain controls our senses, movements, thoughts, and emotions. But how? How does the brain do this?

When the puppeteer pulls on the strings that make the puppet's foot move, that tug is like a message to the foot. The message says, "Move, foot." When the puppeteer pulls on the strings to make the puppet laugh, that tug is like a message that says, "Be happy." The puppeteer is very busy, sending hundreds of messages to make the puppet work.

Your brain is a very busy place, too. Both the top and bottom parts of the brain are always at work, sending billions of messages to and from all the parts of your body, all day and all night. No puppeteer has ever had to work that hard!

Obviously, you don't have strings to connect your brain to each and every part of your body. So how does your brain send these messages? How does it tell your heart to beat or your lungs to breathe? How does it receive messages from your eyes so that you can see and from your ears so that you can hear?

Let's take an even closer look at the way the brain works.

The brain is actually a great mass of billions of nerve cells, or neurons, and fibers which connect these cells. There are other nerve cells and fibers throughout your body. All these nerve cells and fibers together make up your nervous system. This system is your body's message network. Messages to and from the brain travel along this network of nerves.

The neurons in your nervous system have a special job to do. They send and receive messages to and from the brain. Each neuron can receive a message, examine the information in that message, and then decide whether or not to send that message to another neuron. To do this job, the neuron needs three basic parts: dendrites, a cell body, and an axon.

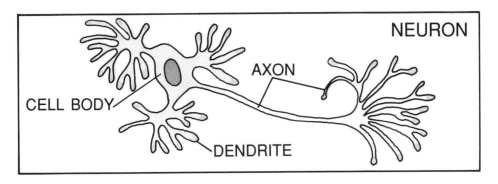

- Dendrites are special branches attached to the cell body. They receive messages from other neurons and send this information to the cell body. Each dendrite is covered with special receptors that are designed to receive messages.

- The cell body is the part of the neuron that examines the messages received by the dendrites. It decides whether the information is important enough to send to another neuron.

- The axon is a long, thin fiber, much like a telephone wire. The special job of the axon is to transmit messages from the cell body of one neuron to the dendrites on a different one.

Messages travel from neuron to neuron, from the axon of one neuron to a dendrite of another neuron. And on and on. But between each neuron and the next one, there is a gap. This gap is called a synapse. A message has to jump across the synapses between neurons. To bridge these gaps, neurons make use of special chemicals called transmitters. The job of these transmitters is to carry a message across the synapses.

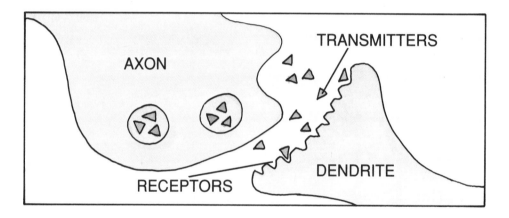

There are many different chemical transmitters at work within the brain, and they carry different kinds of messages. Some transmitters carry the messages that control our senses. They enable us to see and hear the world around us. Some transmitters carry the messages that control the body's movements. They enable us to use our muscles. Some transmitters carry the messages that control our thoughts and emotions. They enable us to understand and react to our world.

34

Each transmitter has its own special shape. You can think of the transmitter as being like a key.

Each receptor also has its own special shape. You can think of the receptor as being like a lock. Only one kind of key fits into each kind of lock.

When the right key fits into the right lock, it opens the pathway of the nervous system. When the right transmitter travels across a synapse and fits into the right receptor, then messages are able to travel along the pathway of the nervous system to and from the brain.

That's how we feel pain.

If you fall and bang your knee, a "pain" message leaves your knee. It has to travel from neuron to neuron to reach the part of your brain that receives pain messages. But for this to happen, it takes a special transmitter to help carry the pain message across the many synapses between nerve cells. The right transmitter (the one that carries the pain message) must fit into the right receptors (the ones that can receive the pain messages) all along the pathway of the nervous system.

When the right keys open the right locks, the message pathway of the nervous system works the way it is supposed to. When the chemical keys that carry pain messages open the locks that receive them, then pain messages are able to get through to the brain.

What happens then?

When the pain message gets through to the brain, you feel the pain. "Ouch!" you shout.

Sometimes, the brain works in a special way to protect people from too much pain. Imagine that someone has been badly injured. The pain is terrible. What does the brain do? It releases a transmitter that blocks pain messages from traveling along the pathway of the nervous system. This special transmitter attaches to the receptors on the nerve cells that receive pain messages. So when pain messages reach those neurons, there is no place for them to go. They are blocked from going on to the brain. So then what happens?

If the pain messages can't get through to the brain, there is no feeling of pain. You don't feel the pain!

The transmitters that protect people from too much pain are called endorphins. Endorphins change the way the brain normally works. One thing they do is "turn off" the neurons that carry pain messages. In this way, they protect us from too much pain.

Endorphins do other things, too. Another thing they do is "turn on" the pleasure center. When these chemicals attach to special receptors in the pleasure center of the brain, we feel happy or content. When endorphins attach to those receptors, the brain sends out the kind of messages that say, "Feel good."

Endorphins are natural chemicals. The brain controls the production of these transmitters. It directs the body to produce just the right amount of endorphins to protect us from too much pain, to turn on the pleasure center, and to do many other things that help to keep us healthy. But the brain only produces them when they are needed. It stops producing them when they are no longer needed.

Scientists discovered the existence of endorphins in 1973. But long before then, they knew that opiates were able to stop pain. In fact, scientists learned about endorphins by studying how opiates act on the brain. They wondered how opiates work to stop pain. How could the juice from the poppy be so powerful? What was the secret power of the opiate drugs? Where would an answer be found?

Opiates and the Brain

The search for an answer to the opiate problem led to the world of the human brain. Scientists discovered that opiates attach to certain receptors in the brain. These places are called opiate receptors. But this knowledge led to a scientific riddle. Why did the brain have special receptors that fit the chemicals found in opiate drugs? Why did the brain have locks that could be opened by the opiate keys? Scientists believed that there had to be a natural purpose for these special receptors.

What was the answer to this riddle?

Some scientists thought that the body must also produce a natural chemical that fit these opiate receptors, a chemical that was made by the brain and that acted like opiates.

That's how endorphins were first discovered. Scientists learned that endorphins attach to the same receptors in the brain that opiate drugs attach to. They work like opiates to block pain and to produce a feeling of pleasure.

Opiate drugs imitate, or act like, the body's own natural endorphins. The name "endorphin" comes from "endogenous morphine," which means "the morphine within the body." In other words, endorphins are like the body's own morphine.

Like the body's natural endorphins, opiate drugs change the way the brain works.

Opiates, like endorphins, are able to act like the keys that fit special locks in the nervous system. They can change how the message network works. Like endorphins, opiates are able to block pain messages.

Also like endorphins, opiates turn on the pleasure center. They help the brain send out messages that say, "Feel good." That's how they give us a feeling of pleasure.

But if opiates are like a natural chemical that the body produces on its own, why are they a problem?

Why is there an opiate problem?

The answer is actually a quite simple one. Endorphins are natural chemicals. Our brains are able to produce these chemicals in the right amount. (It is a very small amount.) The brain controls the amount of endorphins produced in the body. So the body is kept in a chemical balance.

But using opiate drugs is not a normal or natural way to change the way the body and brain work. When opiates are used, the body's natural chemical balance is upset. The body is flooded with an outside chemical.

Changing the brain with opiates can be very dangerous. Drugs can change the brain in ways that nobody can predict. They can change the brain in ways that nobody wants.

Drugs are not a natural or normal way to turn on the pleasure center. They turn on the pleasure center too much. They turn it on too easily and too fast. They change the brain so that it wants the pleasure it gets from drugs more than the pleasure it gets from natural things, like food and sleep.

Opiate users can begin to get more pleasure from drugs than they get from anything else. So they begin to want the pleasure they get from drugs more than anything else. They can become addicted to opiate drugs.

Why would anyone want to change the way the brain works by using opiate drugs? Why would anyone ever risk upsetting the body's chemical balance? Why would anyone want to interrupt the messages to and from the brain?

You already know one reason: to stop pain. Doctors may prescribe morphine to block pain messages from getting to the brain.

Doctors carefully control the amount and the strength of the opiates that they give to their patients. They know that too strong a dose of opiates can be dangerous. But they also know how to use opiates so that there is little chance of danger or addiction. They know that, when used carefully, opiates can be very helpful as medicine.

But there is another reason why some people want to use opiates to change the way the brain works.

Some people use opiates to get "high." They use opiates because they like the strong feeling of pleasure these drugs give them. This feeling of pleasure is called euphoria. Some opiate users say that, after this euphoria has passed, they get a safe and warm feeling, like being wrapped from head to toe in a soft, thick blanket.

But what they don't like is the feeling they get when the effects of opiate drugs wear off. So opiate users want to take the drug again and again. They also need to take more and more. Opiate users quickly develop a tolerance to the effects of these drugs. This means that they need more and more of a drug to change the way they feel. The same amount is no longer able to turn on the pleasure center. What happened? The nerve cells of the brain have gotten used to the drug so that it takes bigger and bigger doses to get the same effect.

Many opiate users say they no longer get any pleasure from their drug habit. They need opiates *not* to feel pleasure, but just to feel *normal*. This need is called dependence. It means that the use of opiates has changed the way the brain works so that it needs opiates just to work normally. Opiate users crave the opiate "high" because they want to return to a normal mood and state of mind. They want to feel the way they felt *before* they started using opiates.

Opiate users also crave these drugs because they want to avoid the feeling they get if they do not use them. When they do not get opiate drugs, they feel very sick. The sick feeling that opiate addicts get when they stop taking these drugs is called withdrawal.

Someone going through withdrawal might feel like the teenage heroin addict who wrote this poem:

> *You'll vomit, you'll cramp, you'll tie in a knot;*
> *Jangling, your nerves will scream for a shot.*
> *The hot chills, the cold sweats, the withdrawal pains,*
> *Can only be stopped by little white grains.*

Withdrawal is painful and frightening. The brain is so used to opiates that it doesn't know how to work without them. Vomiting, painful cramps, chills, and terrible, "jangling" nerves are common withdrawal symptoms. There are many other symptoms, too. An ordinary touch hurts the skin. Sleep becomes impossible. Light hurts the eyes. And even a soft sound seems like a roar.

It gets so bad that an opiate user may do anything to feel normal again. And one way to feel better is to take more "little white grains" of a drug like heroin.

Many addicts continue to use opiates rather than risk the pains of withdrawal. But when they do, they take even greater risks. They risk their good health. They risk the respect and love of their friends and families. They risk losing their jobs or going to jail. And sometimes they even risk their lives for just one more dose.

Why do they take such a risk? Why do they keep using opiates? Why don't they just stop?

They don't stop because they feel that they can't stop. The use of opiates has changed the brain so much that they feel they must have drugs. They feel they have no choice.

They don't stop because they are addicted to opiates.

They don't stop because the opiate problem has become their problem.

Opiates: A History

The lovely opium poppy has been grown for thousands and thousands of years. And it has always created a problem. It is the same problem that you have been learning about in this book: a drug that is helpful can also be harmful. A drug that can be used as a medicine to help people can also be a powerful psychoactive drug used by people to get "high."

Over 6,000 years ago, the Sumerians, in the ancient land of Mesopotamia, chewed on the flowers of the poppy to ease their aches and pains. They must have also felt the poppy's power to produce pleasure because they called the poppy "the plant of joy." The ancient Greeks also praised the poppy and used it to treat many illnesses, including fevers, headaches, dysentery (a disease that causes diarrhea), deafness, poisoning, and even toothaches. They made a mild sleeping potion from the juice of the unripe poppy seedpods. The Greeks called this drink "opos." It's from the word "opos," which means "sap," that we get the word "opium."

Early in the Middle Ages, the knowledge of opiate drugs reached the countries of the Middle East. When Arab traders traveled around the world, they carried this knowledge with them. And wherever they went, they shared what they had learned, spreading far and wide the use of the drug opium. By the 1400s, opium use began to grow across Europe.

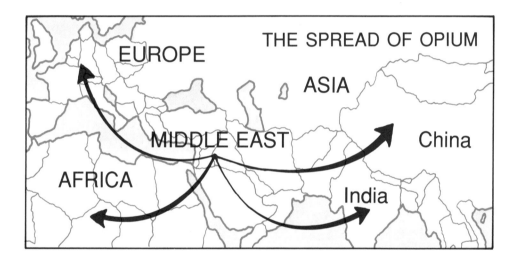

By the 1700s, the use of opiate medicines was widespread. And so was the opiate problem. Every year, ships from India brought tons of opium to the countries of western Europe. New opiate "wonder drugs" were praised everywhere. But it was obvious that these drugs could cause dependence. Tens of thousands of people, from the poor to the wealthy, were soon addicted to opiate medicines.

The opiate problem in China was even worse.

In the seventh century, the Arab traders who first brought opium to Europe arrived in China. They brought with them large quantities of opium. At first, the Chinese used opium mainly as a medicine to control dysentery. Dysentery was a major health problem in China for many years. But over the course of several centuries, hundreds of thousands of Chinese became addicted to opium. By the eighteenth century, there were millions of opium addicts in China.

In 1729, the Chinese government passed very strict laws to control the use of opium. Thousands of users were arrested and sentenced to death. The government also tried to stop other countries from bringing opium into China. But England, which controlled the largest share of the opium trade, refused to stop. The English merchants, bankers, and political leaders were simply not willing to give up the money to be made by importing opium.

The Chinese leaders were afraid that their entire country was going to be destroyed by opium. In March of 1839, they fought back. They destroyed 20,000 chests of opium belonging to the leading English trading company. But this action only led the Chinese into the first of two wars with England. China lost both the Opium War of 1839 and, later, the Opium War of 1856. And England continued to import hundreds of tons of opium into China each year, supplying the drug to millions of Chinese addicts.

Although England won both wars in China, it was losing a major battle at home. Women's groups and church groups protested the English policy of importing opium into China. American missionaries in China also accused England of using opium to destroy the Chinese people. The English authorities were finally forced to listen to these complaints. The opium trade gradually declined. By the 1900s, opium use in China had been greatly reduced.

But before the drug problem was conquered in China, the opium problem was brought to the United States.

In the 1850s and 1860s, thousands of Chinese immigrants came to California to help build the American railroads. They settled along the West Coast, bringing their national customs with them. And one of those customs was smoking opium. Chinese opium dens were soon a common sight in California, and by the 1890s, the Chinese custom of smoking opium was fast becoming an American habit, too. It wasn't long before Americans, too, were becoming addicted to opium. In 1909, the United States government passed its first law restricting the importing of opium.

But opium was only one of the drugs that contributed to opiate addiction in the United States.

In the early 1800s, Friedrich Serturner, a pharmacist from Germany, had discovered a new opiate drug, one that was 10 times stronger than opium. He believed that this drug would be more reliable than opium and safer to use. Serturner named his discovery "morphine" after Morpheus, the ancient Greek god of sleep and dreams. Other scientists continued the search for new opiate drugs. In 1832, a French chemist by the name of Pierre-Jean Robiquet discovered the opiate codeine. In 1874, heroin was discovered by a British scientist, Charles Wright.

By the end of the 1800s, scientists knew the usefulness of opiate drugs. But many of the dangers remained unknown.

There were many reasons why opiates became a major drug problem in this country. Opiates were completely legal drugs in the nineteenth century. Opium poppies were legally imported from abroad and grown at home. Opiate drugs, and the many products made with opiates, were as available as aspirin is today.

And they were just as widely used. Doctors prescribed opiates to many of their patients. Opiate medicines were used routinely to relieve pain and make people calm. In addition, many non-prescription medicines, called "patent" medicines, contained opiates. These opiate medicines could be bought through the mail, at the drugstore, or at the grocery store. Men and women began to use opiate drugs for such everyday ailments as headaches, nervousness, and sleeplessness. They even gave opiates to their babies and children to ease the pain of teething, to treat diarrhea, or just to "soothe their spirits."

Another discovery of the nineteenth century helped to make the opiate drugs more useful as medicine. In 1853, the hypodermic syringe was invented. In 1858, a Scottish doctor, Alexander Wood, showed how the syringe could be used to inject a strong dose of morphine directly into the bloodstream.

In the 1860s, American doctors were given a chance to learn how useful morphine injections really were. This was the period of the American Civil War (1861-1865). It was a horribly bloody war. It took the lives of over 500,000 young men. The new weapons of war inflicted painful wounds on hundreds of thousands of other young men. But now there was a new weapon in the war against pain. It was morphine. Morphine injections were given to the wounded soldiers to ease their pain and keep them calm.

But this new weapon in the war against pain inflicted another kind of injury on many of the wounded soldiers. They often became addicted to morphine. In fact, so many Civil War soldiers became addicted to this opiate that morphine addiction was called "the soldier's disease."

Alexander Wood had hoped that the development of the syringe would reduce the dangers of using opiate medicines. But like other scientists and doctors who sought better opiate medicines, Wood didn't fully understand the opiate problem. Taking opiate drugs by injection increases their strength and the risk of addiction. Although the hypodermic syringe was a major contribution to the world of health and medicine, it also became a major contribution to the problem of opiate addiction. And, sadly, Wood's own wife became addicted to morphine injections. She died a morphine addict.

What was the result of this widespread use of opiates?

By the 1900s, there were hundreds of thousands of opiate addicts in the United States. They were addicted to opium. They were addicted to morphine. And they were addicted to the newer, more powerful, and even more addictive opiate drug, heroin.

In 1906, the United States government passed the Federal Pure Food and Drug Act. This law said that any medicines containing opiates had to be plainly labeled and had to warn people of the possibility of addiction. Then, the United States passed the Harrison Narcotic Act of 1914. This law made it a crime to make, sell, or use any drug that might lead to opiate addiction. All narcotics had to be labeled and could be used only for research or medical purposes.

By the end of the 1960s, there were more than 700,000 heroin addicts in the United States. Although the number of addicts dropped sharply in the early 1970s, it is estimated that, today, there are 500,000 to 750,000 addicts in the United States.

Today, heroin is the opiate problem. Nine out of every 10 opiate addicts use heroin.

People who use heroin take a terrible risk. But the heroin problem is not just a problem for drug users. Heroin use hurts everyone. It even hurts people who would never use drugs. People who use drugs like heroin put everyone at risk.

Let's take a look at the risks of addiction.

The Risks of Addiction

When you close your eyes to go to sleep at night, what do you think about?

You close your eyes and look forward to tomorrow. You hope it will be a good day. You hope it will be a happy day.

Here is what a heroin addict says he thinks about at night:

I close my eyes and get ready for another lousy day. I can't see an end to the routine, unless I don't wake up tomorrow.

An addict's life is not about tomorrow. It is not about hope. An addict's life is about getting and using drugs.

Being addicted to heroin means that only opiate drugs turn on the pleasure center. It means that heroin addicts find pleasure only in drugs. They feel that they must have drugs. They feel that they have no choice. They are driven by their own need for drugs. Being addicted to heroin means giving up tomorrow. It means giving up hope. It means giving up family and friends, education and goals, health and freedom.

A heroin addict turns over control of his or her life to heroin. Heroin becomes the puppeteer, pulling all the strings and telling the user what to do. But heroin is a cruel and heartless puppeteer. Heroin makes the user take unhealthy, dangerous, and even life-threatening risks.

Heroin changes the people who use it. It changes the way they feel. It changes the way they act. Heroin addicts may feel nervous, angry, or depressed. Heroin addicts no longer care about family and friends. They no longer care about school or work. They no longer care about anything—except heroin.

Heroin addicts no longer care about the health risks of addiction. But they should. Heroin is a very dangerous and sometimes deadly drug.

Heroin changes the way the brain works. It slows down, or depresses, the way messages are sent to and from the brain. There are opiate receptors in the part of the brain that controls our breathing. That's why too strong a dose of heroin, also called a drug overdose, can shut down those messages from the brain that direct the lungs to keep breathing. And that's why thousands of drug addicts die every year from heroin overdoses.

Heroin addicts don't eat well. They may not be interested in food, or they may crave only sweets. It's not unusual for heroin addicts to go for days without eating any nutritious food. Because of this, many of them suffer from malnutrition. Heroin can also shut down the movements of the intestines, making it even harder for heroin users to get the nutrients they need to stay healthy.

A heroin user no longer feels pain in the normal way. Opiates prevent pain messages from reaching the brain. This can be helpful for a person who has a painful illness or injury. But it can be dangerous, too. Pain is a set of signals from the brain that tell us something is wrong with the body. These signals alert us to the need for help. But heroin users may not get these pain signals. They may not know when they are hurt or sick. By the time they realize they need a doctor, it may be too late for them to get proper treatment.

Some heroin addicts sniff the drug in a powdery form. This can damage the lining of the nose. The membranes in the nose turn bright red and bleed. In very bad cases, the skin between the nostrils may completely wear away.

But most heroin addicts want to get "high" as quickly as they possibly can. They use a needle to inject, or "shoot," a dose of heroin directly into their veins. This is often called "mainlining." The results are immediate and powerful. But the dangers are tremendous. Addicts may use the same vein over and over again. This can cause the vein to get infected or to collapse. Then, the user must search for another vein— and another and another. The needle holes leave a long trail of ugly scars on the skin. These are known as "track marks."

Addicts often don't care if the needle they use is dirty or if someone else has used it before them. And dirty needles can cause blood poisoning and other diseases. Addicts who share needles run the risk of getting infectious diseases like hepatitis, tetanus, and AIDS. But even this doesn't stop most addicts from using drugs or sharing needles. As one addict said, "I knew that I was bound to get AIDS. But when you're on drugs, that's your whole world."

A dose of heroin contains other substances besides heroin. There may be as little as 3% pure heroin or as much as 20%

pure heroin in a dose. A user has no way of knowing how strong a certain batch of heroin is. Heroin that is stronger than what the user normally takes may lead to an overdose.

Most heroin addicts use other drugs, too. They may use drugs like cocaine when they can't get heroin. They may even mix heroin with other harmful drugs. Some addicts inject a sometimes deadly mixture of heroin and cocaine. This practice is called "speedballing."

But most addicts don't care or worry about dying. They have only one care. They have only one worry. They only care or worry about where their next dose of heroin is coming from. And if addicts don't care about themselves, how can they care about other people? They can't, and they don't.

Who are these heroin users? Some people who feel that they are trapped in a world of poverty and crime try to escape into the world of a heroin "high." But heroin is not just a drug problem for the poor. It is a drug that hurts the rich and the poor. It is a drug problem for people from every race, for male and female, young and old. Did you know that almost 10% of heroin addicts are between the ages of 12 and 17?

You may wonder what kind of person would be willing to trade good health and the love and the care of family and friends for drugs. What kind of person would risk going to jail for drugs? What kind of person is willing to risk dying for drugs?

Profile of a Heroin Addict

Honey, before you start fooling with me,
Let me tell you how it will be.
I shall succeed and make you my slave,
Those stronger than you have gone to the grave.

Those are strong words, aren't they? They're from a poem in which the drug heroin speaks to a person who is thinking about trying it. The writer of the poem was an 18-year-old heroin addict. She wrote the poem while she was in jail.

Addicts don't learn how to face problems without drugs. They use drugs to run away from life. They usually drop out or fail out of school. They usually can't keep a job. But drugs are expensive. Heavy heroin users might need anywhere from $50 to $150 a day to pay for their habits. Without a job, how can they get their drug money?

Often, they steal it. They steal from their families. They steal from their friends. Or they commit other crimes to get money. Many addicts become drug dealers. The courts and jails are filled with heroin users arrested for selling drugs.

There are hundreds of thousands of heroin addicts in the United States today. Here is the story of one of them.

She ran away from home when she was 13. Out on the streets, she started using drugs—whatever drugs she could get, including heroin. Soon, she was addicted to heroin. Like most addicts, she lived for the pleasure of the heroin "high." But, eventually, she took it just to avoid the pain of heroin withdrawal. She was a slave to heroin. And she seemed to be willing to suffer anything for it.

Once, after she used a dirty needle, her leg got infected. It almost had to be cut off. But that didn't stop her. As soon as she was out of the hospital, she began using heroin again. Her mother tried to help her. But it was no use. She stole money from her mother and returned to the street.

At 21, she was unmarried and pregnant. Her baby was born addicted to heroin. This often happens to babies born to heroin users. Hours after its birth, her baby girl started to go through withdrawal. The doctors worried that her baby might have been born with brain damage. They were afraid that her baby girl might die.

She tried to stop taking drugs so that she could care for her baby. But, in the end, the baby didn't matter. Only heroin mattered. She left her baby and went back to the streets. She turned her back on all the things she cared about. She turned to the only thing she really cared about. She turned to heroin.

People who use heroin are taking a terrible risk. But they are not the only ones who are at risk. They are not the only ones hurt by drugs like heroin. We all are.

Drug use can destroy a family. People who use heroin can no longer be trusted. They are difficult to talk to. They may be sad or angry for no reason. And they often deny that there is a drug problem to begin with. Other family members may feel that there is nothing they can do to help. They may stop trying. Or they may start looking the other way.

Drug use can destroy a neighborhood. Opiates are illegal to buy and sell except as prescription medicines. When an addict or anyone else buys drugs from a dealer, it helps to keep the illegal drug business operating. Drug dealers make a lot of money selling drugs. But they are criminals, and they will not hesitate to use violence to carry on their business. This violence often spills out onto the streets where innocent people can be hurt. You may have read newspaper stories of people wounded or killed in the crossfire of drug dealers.

Drug use can even hurt babies before they are born. When a pregnant woman uses heroin, her unborn baby gets a dose of the drug. Each year, thousands of babies are born addicted to heroin. They have to go through the painful stages of drug withdrawal. And they may suffer long-term effects, too. These babies may learn more slowly than other children. They may have a hard time getting along with other people.

Heroin is a drug that hurts everyone, even those who would never use it. One way or another, the heroin problem affects every one of us. Today, the United States is waging an international war against the people who smuggle drugs like heroin into this country and sell them on the streets.

The United States government spends almost $6 billion a year to fight the drug trade in this country. It is estimated that soon the war on drugs may cost the United States over $10 billion each year. Where does the money come from to wage a war against drugs? It comes from money that could be spent on education, or housing, or health care. So everyone ends up paying for drug abuse.

Treatment and Recovery

For as long as people have been using opiate drugs, doctors and scientists have searched for ways to help treat addiction.

Today, there are several ways to treat addiction to heroin. One kind of treatment uses the drug methadone. Methadone can stop withdrawal pains and the craving for heroin without providing the pleasure that heroin does. After three or four weeks of taking methadone, most addicts are no longer dependent on heroin.

But many addicts don't stay in a treatment program long enough to be cured. Even those who do complete a drug program often start to use heroin again. They go back to their old lives and their old problems. They go back to their old drug habits. Less than 15% of the heroin addicts who seek treatment actually recover.

Drugs like methadone are only the first step toward recovery from heroin addiction. Addicts need continued counseling and education. They need to learn how to deal with problems—without drugs. They need to learn how to face life—without drugs. They need to be able to look in the mirror and say, "I don't need drugs to be happy."

Opiates and You

How can you keep the opiate problem from becoming your problem?

First, you need to remember that some opiate drugs can be very useful medicines.

Should you be afraid of medicines that contain opiates? No. You know that drugs like codeine and morphine can help you get better.

Should you worry about becoming addicted to drugs like codeine and morphine? No. You know that when doctors use opiates as medicines, there is very little risk of addiction.

Second, you need to remember that opiates are strong drugs. You know that you should never use them on your own. You know it would be dangerous.

But sometimes young people do things they know are dangerous. They may forget about the risks. Or they may not worry about them. Some young people use drugs even though they know how dangerous they are.

Why?

Why do young people use drugs even when they know the risks?

Some young people use drugs to escape. They may use drugs to escape from the pressures of growing up. Growing up is not always such an easy thing to do. At times, young people may feel lonely, afraid, and confused. They may not feel sure of themselves. They may ask, "Am I smart enough?" Or, "Am I pretty enough?" Or, "Am I popular enough?"

For some young people, drugs seem like an answer to these questions. It may seem that drugs can help them escape to a place where they feel confident and happy.

But using drugs doesn't get rid of problems. It only makes them worse. People who use drugs to escape their problems may never learn how to solve problems without drugs. They may turn to drugs whenever they face a difficult time. They may soon find out that they have a drug problem, too.

Some young people give in to another kind of pressure. They give in to peer pressure. Peer pressure is when you do something to be one of the crowd. It means doing something to fit in with other kids. The other kids may want you to try out for a certain sport, or see a certain movie, or wear a certain style of clothes. Peer pressure is a natural part of growing up. Everyone wants to be like other kids. Everyone wants to be liked by other kids.

But can you say "No" to peer pressure when you really want to? Can you say "No" if you are being pressured to do something you think is dangerous or wrong? Can you say "No" if you are pressured to use drugs?

The answer is "Yes!" Most kids say "No" to the pressure to use drugs. They know that real friends would never ask them to use drugs. Most kids never use drugs. They never start, so they don't have to stop.

You can say "No," too. And not just to opiate drugs. Most heroin addicts started out using other drugs, like marijuana or alcohol. Drugs like marijuana and alcohol are sometimes called "gateway" drugs. These drugs can "open the gate" to drug problems. You can say "No" to these drugs, too!

You can say "No" to harmful drug use. You can keep the gate shut on drug problems. You can say "Yes" to yourself, your family, and your friends. And you can open the gate to a healthy, happy, and drug-free life.

Glossary

addict   a person who is addicted to a drug or drugs

addiction   the constant need or craving that makes people use drugs they know are harmful

codeine   one of several opiate drugs

dealer   a person who sells illegal drugs

dependence   the way the body and brain need a drug to avoid feeling sick

endorphin   a kind of chemical, produced within the body, that acts on the brain like opiate drugs

euphoria   a feeling of great pleasure; a term used to describe one of the effects of opiates

"fix"   a slang term for a dose of heroin

gateway drug   a drug that can lead to other drug problems

heroin   one of several opiate drugs

hypodermic needle   a medical instrument used to inject fluids through the skin into the body

"junk"   a slang term for heroin

"junkie"   a slang term for a heroin addict

"mainlining"	injecting a dose of a drug into the bloodstream with a hypodermic needle
methadone	a drug that is used in the treatment of heroin addiction
morphine	one of several opiate drugs
narcotics	another word for the opiate drugs
opiate	a kind of psychoactive drug that is made from the juice of the opium poppy
opium	one of several opiate drugs
opium poppy	a flower that is the source of the opiate drugs; *Papaver somniferum*
overdose	too strong a dose of a drug, leading to illness, injury, or death
peer pressure	the feeling that you have to do something because other people your age are doing it
psychoactive drug	a substance that acts on the brain to change thoughts, feelings, and behavior
"speedballing"	injecting a dose of heroin and cocaine
tolerance	the way the body and brain need more and more of a drug to get the same effect
withdrawal	the sick feeling drug users get when they can't get the drugs they are dependent on

Index